I miss all of you,
my world is
just not right.

Turning upside-down right side up...by connecting with the other side

# Turned Upside Down

written by: Teana Taché
illustrated by: Karen Keesler

Thank you to my husband Eli for your unconditional support. To my sons Jeremy and Jason for embracing Turned Upside Down with excitement and love. To my friends and family for your encouragement and foresight. To Sally for my very special message. To Karen for a journey too good to be true. To Laura for believing in me from the beginning. To Laya for your special magic. And a very special thank you to Morey for your guidance and wisdom from the other side!
All my love, T

To all of my angels, both here and departed, I thank you.
You have touched my heart in such a special way.
You've taught me strength, given me inspiration and, most importantly, shaped my life with your love!!! Thank you!!

I could not be without the love of my family.
Thank you for your endless patience and unconditional love.
I love you guys. K


Design and layout by Omar Garcia
Printed in the United States of America



All inquiries should be addressed to
tache@foureverafter.com

My Dearest

______________________________,

Name of your special someone

My world has turned

upside down and I miss you.

I miss your voice
on the other side
of the phone.

I miss your big hugs
when you would
come home.

I miss
the way
you would
hold my
hand.

I miss our talks,
I just don't understand.

I miss your smile, the way
it made me feel safe and sound.

I feel
lost now,
like I will
never be
found.

I miss your kiss before
I go to sleep at night.

Turning upside-down right side up...by connecting with the other side

The space below is for you to write your thoughts, memories and feelings.

________________________________________

________________________________________

________________________________________

________________________________________

________________________________________

________________________________________

________________________________________

Enjoy your journey... it's not The End.

Name: ____________________ Date: __________ Age: _______

Turned Upside Down
is dedicated to my brother, Morey.

Morey, I love you, why did you have to leave - I wanted to know.
I did not understand why you had to go.
At first I did not want to believe.
I asked why you and then why me.
I have grown older - my desire to know you has grown deep.
Curiosity has taken over the sadness, I no longer weep.
I realize things happen for a reason, no specific
time, place or season.
My dearest brother Morey,
You are always in my heart, with warm and loving thoughts,
I continue to live my life with you as a very big part.

- Teana Taché, 1981, age 15

I will be there
deep down inside.
I will always be here,
right by your side.

This is where
I will stay
a very, very
big part.

Today, tomorrow and always,
our love will live in your heart.

It's okay to talk about me,
to laugh and to cry.

It is even okay
to question why.

The more
you do, the more
we will once again fit.

Share your
life with me,
every last little bit.

So close your eyes
again, remember me-
and all the things
we would say and do.

I know you can not see me,
or hear me, the way that
you knew.

What is a soul and a
spirit you ask?
They are the parts of us
that will always last.

It's important
to know and always
remember, my soul
and my spirit will
stay forever.

I know your
whole world
feels so
very wrong.

I Know it is hard
to understand
why I have gone.

So close your eyes
and feel my love
for you.

I know that you miss me and I miss you too.

My Dearest

______________________________,

Your name

Believe. Love. Remember.